Floss Your Teeth!

my healthy habits

Published in the United States of America by Cherry Lake Publishing
Ann Arbor, Michigan
www.cherrylakepublishing.com

Reading Adviser: Marla Conn MS, Ed., Literacy specialist, Read-Ability, Inc.
Book Design: Jennifer Wahi
Illustrator: Jeff Bane

Library of Congress Cataloging-in-Publication Data

Names: Marsico, Katie, 1980- author. | Bane, Jeff, 1957- illustrator.
Title: Floss your teeth! / by Katie Marsico ; [illustrator] Jeff Bane.
Description: Ann Arbor, Michigan: Cherry Lake Publishing, [2019] | Audience: K to grade 3. | Includes bibliographical references and index.
Identifiers: LCCN 2018034524| ISBN 9781534142770 (hardcover) | ISBN 9781534140530 (pdf) | ISBN 9781534139336 (pbk.) | ISBN 9781534141735 (hosted ebook) Subjects: LCSH: Teeth--Care and hygiene--Juvenile literature. | Dental care--Juvenile literature. Classification: LCC RK63 .M368193 2019 | DDC 617.6/01--dc23 LC record available at https://lccn.loc.gov/2018034524

Printed in the United States of America
Corporate Graphics

table of contents

About the author: Katie Marsico is the author of more than 200 reference books for children and young adults. She lives with her husband and six children near Chicago, Illinois.

About the illustrator: Jeff Bane and his two business partners own a studio along the American River in Folsom, California, home of the 1849 Gold Rush. When Jeff's not sketching or illustrating for clients, he's either swimming or kayaking in the river to relax.

Photo Credits: ©Sergey Novikov/Shutterstock, 5; ©Vadim Martynenko/Shutterstock, 7; ©Jacek Chabraszewski/Shutterstock, 9; ©TY Lim/Shutterstock, 11; ©Studio KIWI/Shutterstock, 13; ©Lucky Business/Shutterstock, 15; ©Shane Trotter/Shutterstock, 17; ©p_ponomareva/Shutterstock, 19; ©Jacob Lund/Shutterstock, 21; ©wavebreakmedia/Shutterstock, 23; Cover, 6, 8, 16, Jeff Bane; Various vector images throughout courtesy of Shutterstock.com/Irina Iglina and Macrovector

Smile!

When we do, people see our teeth.

But do they see everything?

Each tooth has five **surfaces**.

They aren't all easy to see.
Some aren't easy to reach.

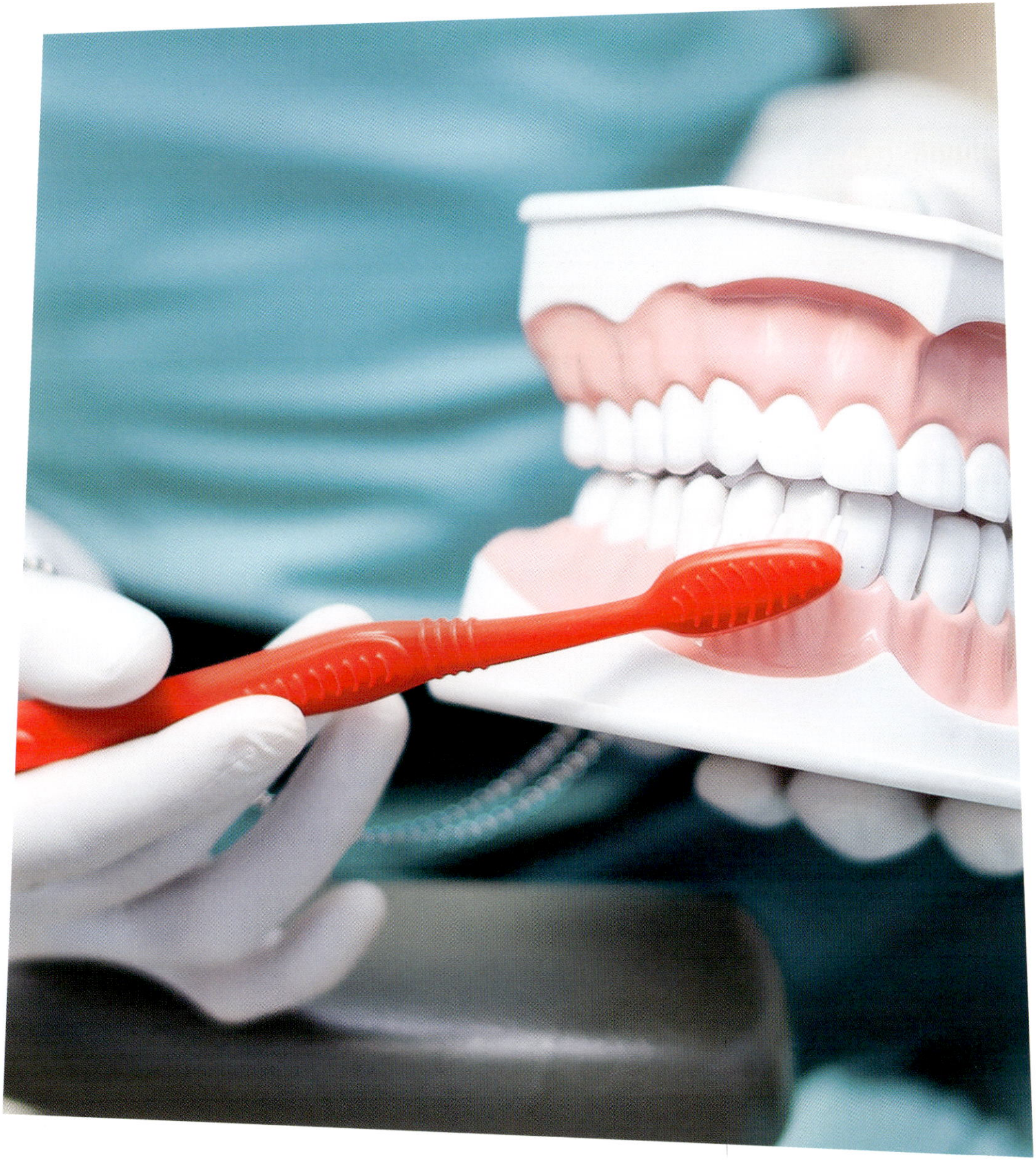

A toothbrush does not fit everywhere.

Brushing only cleans part of each tooth.

How often do you brush your teeth?

Food gets stuck between teeth. It forms **plaque**.

Plaque leads to **cavities**. It hurts our **gums**, too.

That's why we floss!

Good **hygiene** keeps our mouth clean.

Flossing is part of good hygiene.

Floss is soft string. People move it between their teeth.

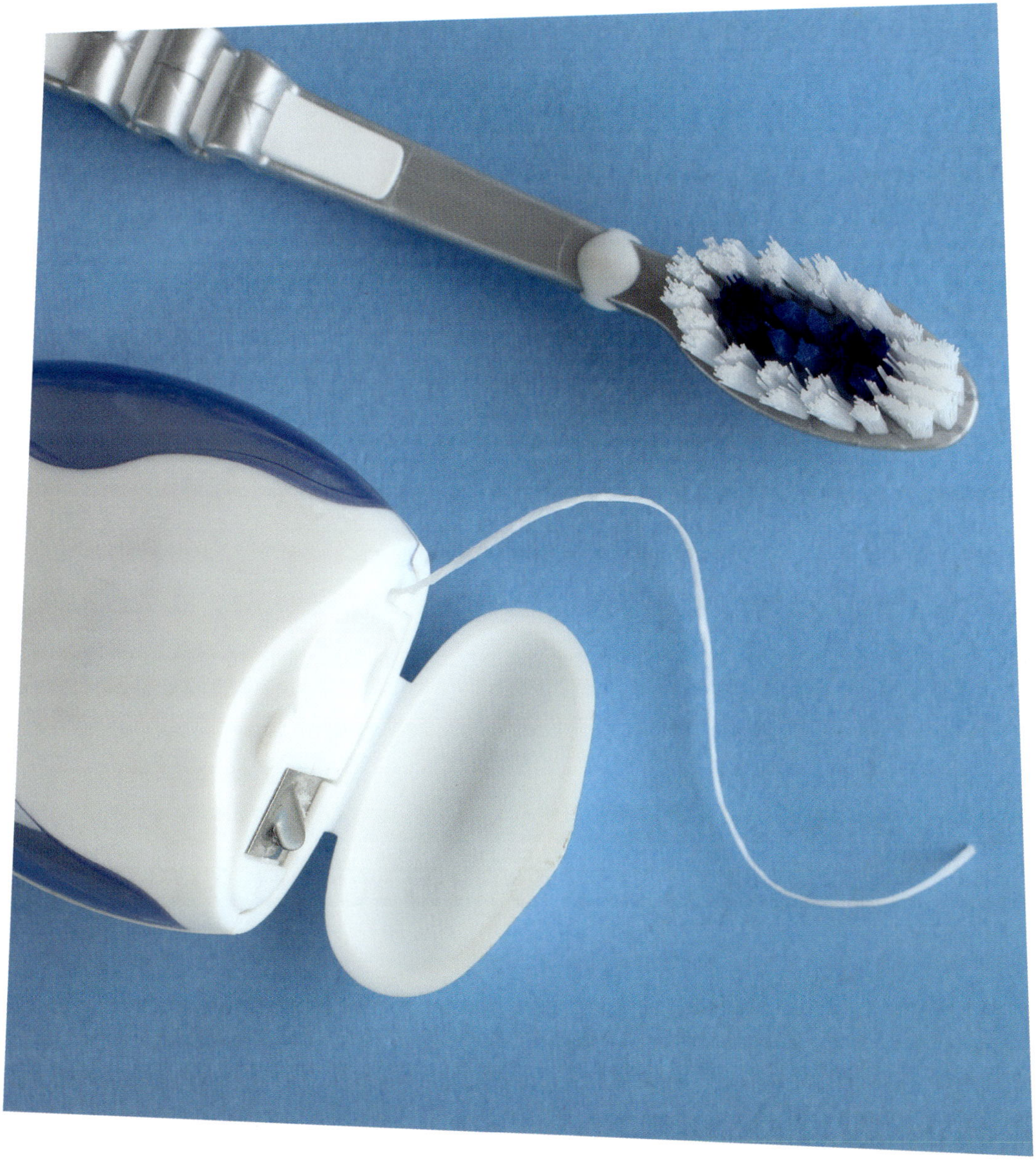

Dentists explain how to floss.

People should floss at least once a day.

What's your favorite part about going to the dentist?

Some people use floss holders.

Others hold the floss in their fingers.

Be sure to tear off enough floss. It should wrap around your **index finger** and middle finger.

Begin at the back of your mouth.

Slowly move toward the front.

Slide the floss between two teeth.

Start flossing when you reach the gum.

Push and pull the floss against each tooth.

Move the floss up and down in the spaces between the teeth.

Throw the floss away when you're done.

Flossing protects your whole mouth.

Brushing alone isn’t enough.

You need to floss to keep your smile healthy!

What are some of your healthy habits?

glossary

cavities (KAH-vuh-teez) areas where teeth have rotted away

gums (GUHMZ) areas of firm, pink flesh that cover parts of the teeth and inner jaw

hygiene (HYE-jeen) keeping yourself clean or other actions that support good health

index finger (IN-dehks FIN-guhr) the finger closest to your thumb

plaque (PLAK) a soft, sticky film on teeth that contains bacteria

surfaces (SUHR-fuhs-uz) the outside or outermost layers of something

index